ALL ABOUT
Coding Selections

BY GEORGE ANTHONY KULZ

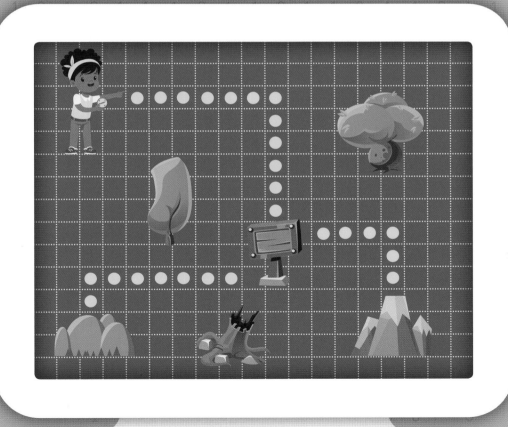

Published by The Child's World®
1980 Lookout Drive • Mankato, MN 56003-1705
800-599-READ • www.childsworld.com

Photographs ©: Notion Pic/Shutterstock
Images, cover (girl), cover (trees), cover (sign),
cover (stump), cover (hill), cover (mountain),
1 (girl), 1 (trees), 1 (sign), 1 (stump), 1 (hill), 1
(mountain), 4, 8, 18, 24; Shutterstock Images,
5, 12; Best Backgrounds/Shutterstock Images,
9; Iryna Tiumentseva/Shutterstock Images,
15; Hung Chung Chih/Shutterstock Images,
16; Redpixel.pl/Shutterstock Images, 19

ISBN 9781503831971
LCCN 2018962818

Printed in the United States of America
PA02418

ABOUT THE AUTHOR

George Anthony Kulz holds a master's degree in computer engineering. He is a member of the Society of Children's Book Writers and Illustrators and has taken courses at the Institute of Children's Literature and the Gotham Writers Workshop. He writes for children and adults.

TABLE OF CONTENTS

CHAPTER 1

What Is a Selection?

Maxine and Philip are hiking in the woods. They have a map, but they did not plan their route before they started. They reach a fork in the path. Should they go left or right? They know they must be home in two hours.

Maxine and Philip use a map to know which path to choose. Computers have their own kind of map that helps them make choices, too.

5

According to the map, the path on the left would take them over a small hill and back to the house. The view from the hill would be nice, but the map says it would take three hours to get home. The path on the right would take them by the river. It would take one and a half hours to get home that way. They choose to take the path on the right. This path will get them home in time.

Maxine and Philip chose which path to take. Computers also need to make choices. Computers make choices using **selections**.

Here is what Maxine and Philip's choice would look like as a selection.

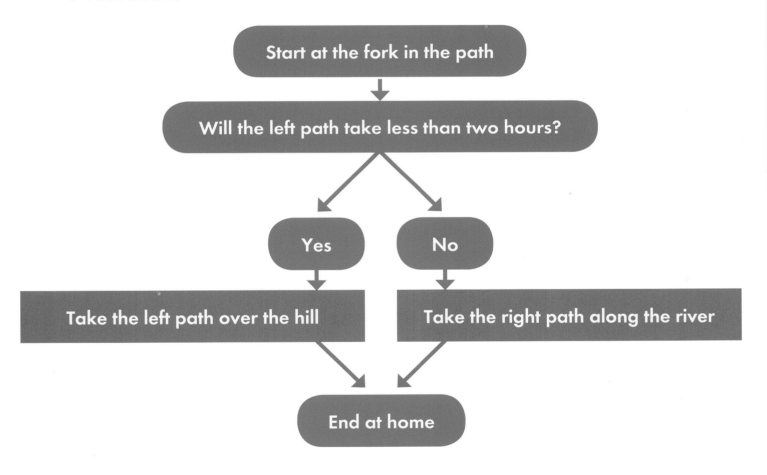

CHAPTER 2

Selections in Code

Computers cannot make choices without **code**. Code is a set of steps that tell a computer what to do. Sometimes these steps are simple **sequences**. A sequence is a list of steps that are done in a certain order. Other times, the code has to make a choice, just as Maxine and Philip did when planning their route. This type of code is called a selection.

```
                              "unread-icon")
         } else;
if (t.hasOwnProperty("unread_notifs"))
      if (global.data.unread_notifs != t.
          global.data.unread_notifs = t.u
          var a = $(".mmi-notif .hri-msg"
          a.html(t.unread_notifs), t.unre
                "unread-icon")
      } else;
)
```

Selections are parts of code that let computers make choices.

```
ion clear_moreoptions_row(t) {
                lass("inp_modified"), t.hasCla
```

Most selections have the same three parts: *if*, *then*, and *else*. The *if* is a **condition**. A condition is either true or false. Conditions can be stated in the form of a question. The condition for Maxine and Philip's route home is "Will the left path take less than two hours?" If the answer is yes, then the condition is true. If the answer is no, then the condition is false.

The *then* and the *else* are the choices that the computer can make. In a selection, each choice has a different set of code steps connected to it. When the condition is true, the computer follows the *then* code. When the condition is false, it follows the *else* code.

```
if (condition_is_true) {
     run_this_code      --This is the then code.
} else {
     run_this_other_code     --This is the else code.

}
```

In the example above, the *if* marks the beginning of the selection. The condition goes between parentheses. The *then* and *else* code go between curly braces. The *then* and *else* are the choices that the computer can make.

Computers use selections to choose whether to end computer games.

Suppose a computer game gives a player three lives. When the player loses a life, the game subtracts one from the total. The computer must then make a choice each time a life is lost. The condition asks the question "Is the player's number of lives greater than zero?" If the number of lives left is greater than zero, the computer will choose to run the code that continues the game. This is the *then* code. If the number of lives left equals zero, the computer will choose to run the code that ends the game. This is the *else* code. As long as there are lives left, the player gets to keep playing.

CHAPTER 3

Many Different Choices

A selection can have many different choices. For example, in a computer game there are different ways to earn points. When players earn points, the game displays different messages. Scoring a goal causes one message to be displayed. Assisting another player causes a different message to be displayed. Saving a ball from going in the goal causes a third message to be displayed. Each time the player earns points, the computer must decide which code will display the right message.

Selections let computers choose
what to display in a game.

If a coder does not write code for all of the possible choices, the program could crash. Then it cannot be used.

16

Computers can only do what code tells them to do. When a **coder** writes a selection, the code must include steps for every possible choice. Forgetting to put all of the possible choices in the computer code could make the computer do strange things. For example, if a coder forgets to have a character stop walking when it hits a wall, the character might walk through the wall. This could **crash** the game.

Selections are an important part of writing code. They allow the computer to make choices about which steps to take. Without selections, computers would not be able to do as many tasks. When used correctly, selections can be powerful coding tools.

Coders use selections to make computers do more.

Q: Which word means a set of steps that are done in order?

    a. selection

    b. condition

    c. sequence

    d. none of the above

A: c. sequence

Q: What are the three parts of a selection?

A: The three parts of a selection are the *if*, or condition, the *then*, and the *else*.

Q: What happens when all possible choices are not accounted for in a selection?

A: The program could crash, or the computer could do strange things.

Q: True or false? A selection can only have two choices.

  a. true

  b. false

A: b. false. A selection can have as many choices as a coder writes in the code.

GLOSSARY

code (KOHD) Code is a list of instructions that computers follow to do things. Coders write code that helps computers solve problems.

coder (KOHD-ur) A coder is someone who writes code. A coder creates computer games.

condition (kun-DISH-uhn) A condition is something that is needed before a set of code can run. In a game, the code has the condition that the player must have lives left to keep playing.

crash (KRASH) To crash means to stop working. When computer games crash, people cannot keep playing them.

selections (suh-LEK-shunz) Selections are the type of code that computers use to choose between different options. A coder uses selections to tell the computer which messages to display in the game.

sequences (SEE-kwunss-ez) Sequences are sets of simple steps in code that must be followed in order. A computer can solve math problems by using different sequences of code steps.

IN THE LIBRARY

Dickins, Rosie. *Lift-the-Flap Computers and Coding*. London, UK: Usborne, 2015.

Scott, Marc. *A Beginner's Guide to Coding*. New York, NY: Bloomsbury, 2017.

Woodcock, Jon. *Coding with Scratch Workbook*. New York, NY: DK Publishing, 2015.

ON THE WEB

Visit our website for links about coding:
childsworld.com/links

Note to Parents, Teachers, and Librarians: We routinely verify our
Web links to make sure they are safe and active sites.
So encourage your readers to check them out!

INDEX